IN SEARCH
Basic K9 Scent T

Lorrie Wnuk

In Search of Scent - Basic K9 Scent Theory Training
© 2009 Lorrie Wnuk

All rights reserved. No part of this book may be reproduced or transmitted in any form by any means, electronic or mechanical, including photocopying and recording, or by any information storage and retrieval system, except as may be expressly permitted by the 1976 Copyright Act or by the publisher. Requests for permission should be made in writing to Crisis Education Systems LLC, 1046 Lememrs Road, Casper, Wyoming 82601.

Illustrations by Lorrie Wnuk and Roy Engebretson, except as otherwise noted.
Photography by Lorrie Wnuk
Cover photo by Lorrie Wnuk
Book design by Lorrie Wnuk

Manufactured in the United States of America
First Edition

Introduction

What is it? What is the reason that allows us to train dogs to find whatever it is we seem to be seeking? Dogs are an amazing animal with a nose to prove it. There are also the advantages of being able to use this domesticated and loving animal to perform tasks for us just because they love the attention, food or the toy at the end of the task. There really is no greater joy than to watch your dog do what you have trained it to do and do it well.

But how does this work? What is scent theory? Do we really know how and why our dogs do what they do? The word theory means an idea, an opinion in some cases. There is real science behind the structure and abilities of a dogs olfactory but a theory about what they do with that scent is just that, a theory. I have been a search and rescue K9 tracking and trailing handler for over 10 years and have been shown and made a believer out of a scent theory that works, and works well, not just on some dogs but all dogs I have worked with.

In this book I will present what I was taught, what I have found to be realistic and workable and what can help you train your dog to become a master tracker, trailer, air scent, drug or cadaver dog. The information in this book is also derived from experiences of not only myself but many handlers I have worked with over the years, some in search and rescue and some from law enforcement.

Happy tails,

Lorrie Wnuk

ACKNOWLEDGMENTS

This book would not have been possible without the tremendous efforts of Bob Borden and Roy Engebretson. Without the contributions of these men, my knowledge and this book would have never been complete.

Roy Engebretson is a M.C.A. Level III Master Trainer for the U.S.P.C.A. He is in my opinion one of the best scent theory instructors I have ever had the privilege to tutor under. His many years of police canine training and certifications have brought him to a level of experience that far surpasses most. After having sat through many other scent theory classes taught by various other instructors, I found that none made sense to the level that Roy's did. His scent theory is not only scientifically based, but also common sense based. Roy also teaches the theories of Ken Chiacchia, PhD and author of "In Search of Human Scent" as I make reference to in this book.

Bob Borden is a M.C.A. Master Trainer and Judge for the U.S.P.C.A. I have had the pleasure of training under Bob's direction for the past ten years. Bob also teaches the theories of Ken Chiacchia, PhD and author of "In Search of Human Scent." I have never met anyone who can help you read your dog and know what he is going to do before he does it like Bob does. Bob has a history working canines since he was a young boy beginning with sled dogs, hunting dogs and police canines. His years of experience in handling working dogs has made him not only an excellent trainer, but also in tune with the dogs themselves. Bob has given me the skills to be patient, the confidence to trust my dog and the knowledge to make it all work together.

THE THEORY

Ken Chiacchia PhD, author of "In Search of Human Scent," is a firm believer in scent theory. I heartily agree with his findings on scent theory and have found it to be very useful when training my dogs and helping others establish good working dogs. The use of dogs by humans is a very old technology and not a simple one. Understanding how our canine SAR partners work requires us to understand their sense of smell. Scent research hasn't uncovered anything that would overturn most good-faith training and operational practices of SAR dog teams. And yet, science sometimes surprises us.

Most dog handlers' first exposure to the science of scent came from either *Scent and the Scenting Dog* by Syrotuck (1972) or *Scent* by Pearsall and Verbruggen (1982). While excellent books for their time, both were written before the research findings of the 1980s and 1990s exploded scientific knowledge of scent and the detection and characterization of odors.

In 1991, a team of researchers at Columbia University reported how they had isolated the genes that tell the body how to make olfactory receptors. These receptors are proteins that sit on the surface of specialized nerve cells in the nasal membranes and detect odorants -- specific chemicals that carry odor.

Detection of an odor begins when an odorant molecule sticks to a pocket in an olfactory receptor protein, which in turn signals its nerve cell to fire a message to the brain's olfactory lobe. Each olfactory receptor's "binding site" fits only a small number of odorants of similar molecular shape and chemical properties -- much as a lock fits only keys of a certain shape. (See figure 1.) Many types of receptors with different binding sites gives animals the ability to detect a wide variety of odorants.

Ken says that, interestingly, both humans and dogs appear to have about the same number of olfactory receptor genes: roughly 1,000. However, as many as 75 percent of human olfactory receptor genes are "pseudogenes," which are false genes that don't produce any working receptors. Dogs, which appear to have far fewer pseudogenes than humans, can smell a large number of odors that we can't detect at all.

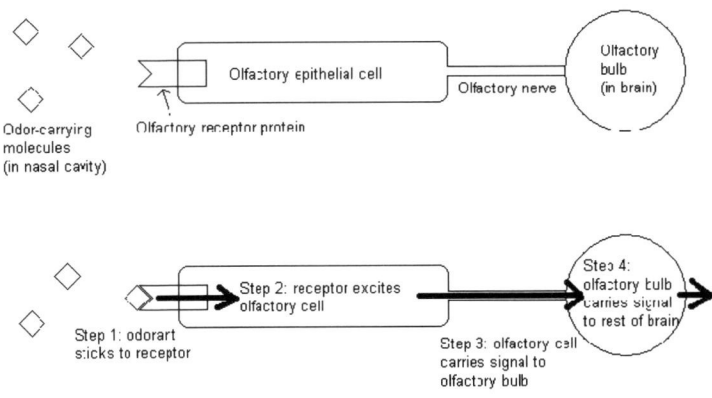

Fig.1: An olfactory receptor will only bind to an odorant that has a complementary shape and chemistry (symbolized here by color). When it does (bottom), it fires a signal that in turn causes its nerve cell to fire a signal to a specific part of the brain's olfactory lobe. (Illustration from "In Search of Human Scent" an article published by Kenneth Chiacchia PhD in Advanced Rescue Technology, October/November 2000, pages 24 to 30.

Olfactory nerve cells with the same receptor type send their signals to the same part of the olfactory lobe. Because of this, different odorant molecules cause different patterns of nerve-cell activity in the brain. A dog's olfactory lobes are larger than ours. We don't fully understand what advantage this gives them. This may contribute to their superior odor-processing, allowing them to pick out faint target odors against a confusing background better than we can.

The next step in the detection of smell is when the brain takes the olfactory lobe activity caused by mixtures of odors and somehow translates it into a unified scent or smell. The same odor can be a part of very different smells. For example, a type of carboxylic acid called L-lactic acid is the primary reason for the sour smell of milk that has gone bad. Accompanied by a different set of other odors, this is a component of the smell of humans. In smaller amounts, it forms part of the pleasant sharpness of some cheeses. Clearly, the way we experience lactic acid depends on both the amount of it present and the other odors we experience at the same time.

An example of this may be found in SAR dog work. Many handlers have observed and described an interesting phenomenon in which a cadaver-trained dog will sniff all around but not approach an especially strong cadaver-scent source. Some handlers wonder if the dog is being overwhelmed by the strength of the source.

Ken Chiacchia guesses that the dogs are being overwhelmed, but in a chemical rather than a behavioral way. When present at high concentrations, an odorant may begin to bind different receptors than it does at lower concentrations.

Therefore, the intense scent at the center of a real cadaver may smell different to the dog than the unavoidably weaker samples she trained on. Fortunately, a properly trained dog will lead the handler quite close if not all the way to the cadaver.

According to Ken, one of the big unanswered questions about how the brain (dog or human) interprets smells is how it combines individual odors into a recognizable, unique scent. In one theory for how this happens (the "keynote" hypothesis), the brain ignores many or even most of the odors coming from a substance, focusing only on certain keynote odors that are unique to that substance.

For instance, a human may smell different from a deer because human body scent contains large amounts of carboxylic acids (from bacterial action on human skin secretions). Our skin also tends to emit traces of non-natural compounds such as hydrocarbon derivatives, because we travel in and refuel vehicles that burn hydrocarbons. Since neither of these are present to any extent in deer scent, all are possible human keynotes.

Another possibility, which Ken calls the "combination lock" hypothesis, is that there are no individual keynote odors that are unique to human scent. Instead, the brain takes a look at *all* the odorants and their relative amounts. The dog identifies human scent when the right proportions of odors exist, although a different combination of the very same odors may say "deer." Finally, dogs may use both keynotes *and* an overall combination to interpret smells.

These hypotheses are important when we consider the use of artificial scent products for training SAR dogs. Say, for instance, we wanted to produce "human scent in a can." Such a product would be useful because in training, we could place it in locations that are hazardous or impossible to place a human being.

If the keynote hypothesis is correct, "human in a can" may be more easily achievable. The only trick would be including all the necessary keynotes without inadvertently putting in false ones. But will the keynotes detected by one dog necessarily be the same keynotes another dog uses?

If combinations are the answer, the task becomes trickier. Not only may it be necessary to pack more individual substances in your can, the proportions of these substances would have to be "right," even after storage. If both keynote and combination are important, would a keynote-style artificial scent be "good enough" to pass small-scale tests but fail in a significant percentage of real-world problems or with certain dogs?

Ken says he does not mean to criticize any specific artificial scent product that may be on the market. In practice, we don't really need to know the composition of an artificial scent product. However, we do need to know how often dogs trained with the artificial human scent alert on scent that isn't human (false positives) and how often they fail to alert on the real thing (false negatives).

In a 1991 paper, researchers from the Savannah River Ecology Laboratory in South Carolina and from Harvard University showed that dogs trained to discriminate between individual humans could not reliably match smells from one part of a person's body to another. For instance, when trained on scent from a person's hand, the dog could not distinguish between scent from that person's elbow crook and from another person's hand. The authors of the study suggested that there might be no such thing as a single individual human scent.

It's important to understand what this experiment *doesn't* show. It doesn't "prove" that our SAR dogs can't trail individual humans. It does, however, suggest that when they do trail individuals, they're doing something far more clever than we realize. When given a hat as a scent article, they may need to pick out the scent from that person's head from those of the rest of his body in order to trail him.

As we have witnessed, many experienced discrimination dog handlers anticipated this scientific finding long ago. For quite some time, it's been common for dog handlers to make a point of using a variety of objects containing human scent while training. The main reason is to ensure the dog learns to pick up scent from any possible scent object. However, it may also train the dogs to pick out scents from different parts of the body and follow them.

A paper published in April, 2000, by researchers at the Monell Chemical Senses Center in Philadelphia and the University of Pennsylvania reviewed discoveries of the 1980s and 1990s about *human*-detectable human body smell. This paper offers interesting clues as to what human scent might be and what our dogs may be doing with it.

The parts of the human body most responsible for what *we* can smell are the armpits and the genital areas. In fact, human infants can identify their mothers via armpit scent alone. Both these areas contain especially rich populations of eccrine sweat glands, which produce moisture; sebaceous glands, which produce oils that bacteria turn into carboxylic acids; and apocrine glands, which produce steroid-like odor molecules similar to those that have been implicated in forming the individual scents of animals. Of the two body areas, the armpits are probably more important, because with normal hygiene the genital area is considerably dryer; and as dog handlers know, moisture is crucial for the bacterial growth that produces much of human scent.

Researchers found that carboxylic acids and odiferous steroids are among the most important parts of human scent. This may be important, because most parts of the body -- lacking apocrine glands especially -- don't produce nearly as much of the scent that comes from *b*acterial action on *a*pocrine/*s*ebaceous/*e*ccrine secretions (which I'll call BASE scent) as the armpits.

You'll recall the 1991 paper showing that dogs couldn't match scent from the hand with the same person's elbow crook. But if BASE scent plays a major role in individual human scents, the dogs may have been trying to match one trace scent with another -- a very difficult task, unless they were trained specifically to do it. When we train our dogs to scent discriminate via a pocketknife touched by the subject, they may not be learning to detect "hand odor." They may be learning to pick up trace amounts of BASE scent on the hands. For this reason, scent articles that contain larger amounts of BASE scent, such as underwear or shirts that have touched the armpits, may be more resistant to contamination than other objects (although this hasn't been proved).

As Ken points out, an important facet of these findings is that pre-pubescent children, who lack apocrine glands, can't have full BASE scent. This obviously doesn't prevent dogs from finding them; but dog handlers whose dogs haven't trained on children sometimes see unusual behavior in their dogs (for example, failure to give a bark signal) when they first encounter children on a search task. It's an argument for using pre-pubescent subjects in training, so that we understand and can work around any quirks in our dog's reactions to incomplete BASE scent.

An article published in February, 2000 by a team from the University of Florida and the U. S. Department of Agriculture's research service used a new method of collecting human skin emanations to create what may be the most complete and exhaustive catalog to date of the volatile molecules that come off human skin. The researchers identified at least 277 chemical compounds that could be potential human odorants. They were careful to say that there are probably more.

Some of these chemical compounds were present in consistent amounts from person to person. Some varied between people. Some varied on a single person from day to day. It would be especially interesting to see if these compounds could be screened to see which of them, or which combinations, search dogs will alert on.

These researchers weren't interested in dogs. They were trying to figure out what mosquitoes use to find humans (it turns out mosquitoes also air scent). However, mosquitoes don't favor human scent over animal to anywhere near the extent that we expect from our dogs. But this research may still provide important clues as to what dogs sense.

Interestingly, mosquitoes do home in on carboxylic acids -- in particular L-lactic acid, the human-body-smell component we discussed earlier. They also home in on carbon dioxide, which we exhale. But they are attracted even more to a *combination* of lactic acid and carbon dioxide. The researchers suspect that, in the real world, mosquitoes home in on a combined profile of odors.

As we can determine, the fact that a compound comes off human skin doesn't necessarily mean it's part of what dogs are smelling. Dogs may not be detecting the same compounds as mosquitoes. But this research does show that an extremely simple organism like a mosquito can use a rather sophisticated combination of signals to home in on hosts. Dogs, which are far more complex, may be capable of far more sophisticated analyses of scent profiles. The research casts a conditional vote for the combination-lock hypothesis, and a cautionary note about whatever artificial scents are likely to be developed in the future.

Scent and the way it is detected is hard to pinpoint, however in the next several pages we will look at the way the nose works, how we emit scent and how it can be effected by environmental factors.

The Study Of Scent

Nasal Plane

The hairless part of the nose, covered with a plaque-like patterning is individual to each dog. It houses the nostrils which serve as the entryway t the large nasal chambers inside. The nostrils are widened during the act of sniffing to draw in larger volumes of air. The ligaments are well developed in mature dogs of the working varieties.

Vomeronasal Organ

The narrow tubular canal, starting near the front part of the nose, behind the K9 tooth, and running along the floor of the nose. It has olfactory cells and many

nerve bundles that connect it directly to the olfactory lobe of the brain. It is felt to
be intimately connected to the olfactory sense. In humans, this organ is very rudimentary and sometimes disappears altogether.

Turbinates
Bony ridges covered with mucous membranes that slow down air movement by protruding into nasal chamber.

Maxillary Turbinates
These have fewer olfactory cells but create turbulence to help heat and moisten the air.

Ethmoturbinates
These are located further back, essentially filling the back half of the nasal chambers, and have the greatest concentration of olfactory receptors. The act of sniffing forces larger volumes of air back over the ethmoturbinates and up the sinus openings which are located in this region.

A cross section of the dog nose and human nose that are approximately proportionate shows the great difference in size of the olfactory areas. Most of the interior of the dog's nose has olfactory tissue compared to the tiny recess at the upper posterior portion of the human nose.

Sinuses
Cavities in the bones of the head which are small at birth and enlarge with age. They are lined with

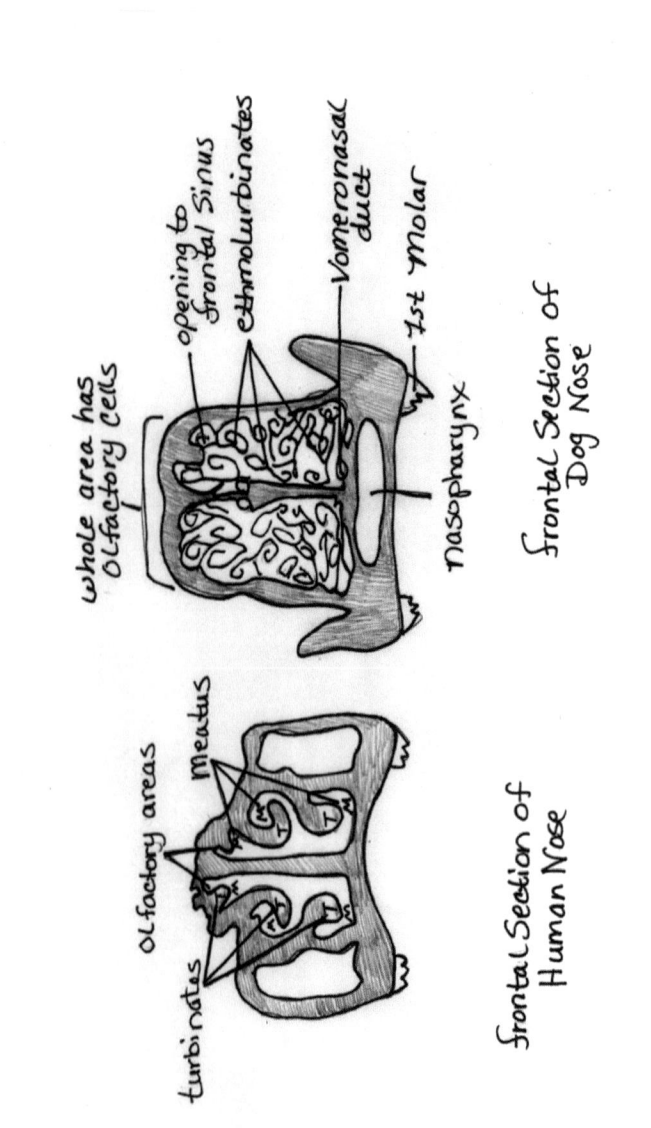

mucous-like cells which may have olfactory capabilities.

Maxillary Sinuses
Located in the roof of the mouth near the roots of the teeth. Infected teeth may involve the sinuses or the vomeronasal gland, thus may seriously impair the ability of the dog to use his nose.

Sephenoid Sinuses
Located in the cheek bones.

Frontal Sinuses
Located in the bones of the forehead and have olfactory cells.

Nerves of Olfaction
These are comparatively large and very numerous. Note the multitude of fine olfactory nerve fibers which cover the ethmoturbinate area. The nerves pass through tiny openings in the bone to go directly to the olfactory lobe.

Olfactory Nerves
The individual cell bodies are located in the mucous membrane of the nose and axons reach up around the base of the cells so that almost every cell in the olfactory epithelium has direct contact with a nerve.

Vomeronasal Nerves
Many fibers unite to form six to eight bundles, then to one to two, which lead directly back to the olfactory

lobe.

Terminal Nerve
Formed of several small bundles of nerves that start from the vomeronasal nerves where they enter the accessory olfactory bulb and lead back along the bulb to connect with the forebrain.

Nasal Mucosa
A mucous membrane covers the whole interior of the nasal chambers. It is made up of several types of cells and secretes a brownish fluid as opposed to the clear fluid in humans. The greatest concentration is toward the front of the nose with occasional olfactory cells interspersed.

Goblet Cells
These cells produce mucous which bathes the whole interior of the nose. It keeps the membranes moist, moistens incoming air, and traps foreign substances. IN the olfactory area it seems to serve as a solvent to trap odorous material.

Olfactory Cells
Olfactory cells (otherwise known as receptor cells) are long narrow cells about six to eight filaments at the upper end that protrude out and float in a mucous layer that covers all the cells. It was felt that the contact between these filaments and odorous substances was the critical factor. These cells are rather sparsely set near the front of the nose and become progressively denser toward the ethmoturbinates where they are very abundant along the sustentacular cells.

Note the very close contact of each cell with the nerve ending.

Sustentacular Cells

These also are long rod-shaped cells with short fibril projections at the top. They seem to have the pigment factors that are responsible for the darker color of the olfactory areas and are as numerous as the receptor cells in the olfactory regions. There is recent evidence to suggest that they may be the more important cells in receiving the odorous substance. In any case, the supporting cells and the receptor cells have a key role in odor sensitivity.

Basal Cells

A layer of cells that underlies both the olfactory areas as well as the mucous areas. They divide regularity, but it is not known quite how they contribute to the cell layers above. The healthy condition of the whole nasal lining is an important factor in scent work. Mucous membranes are easily damaged. It is worth knowing that, in many cases, the nose lining can regenerate after several months, even with some nerve damage.

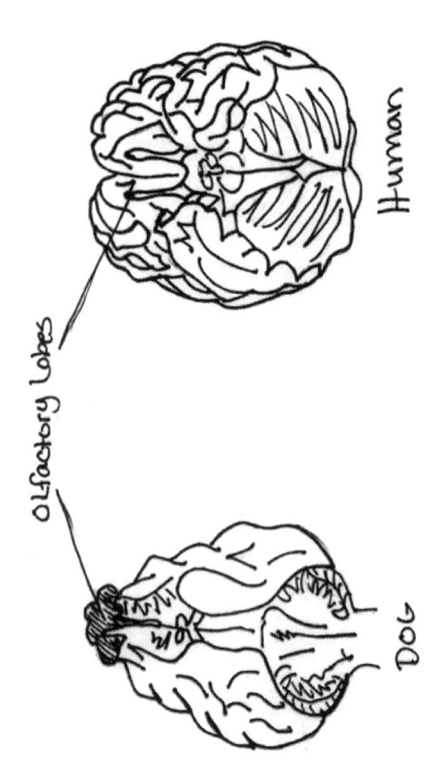

Cross Section of a Dog Nose

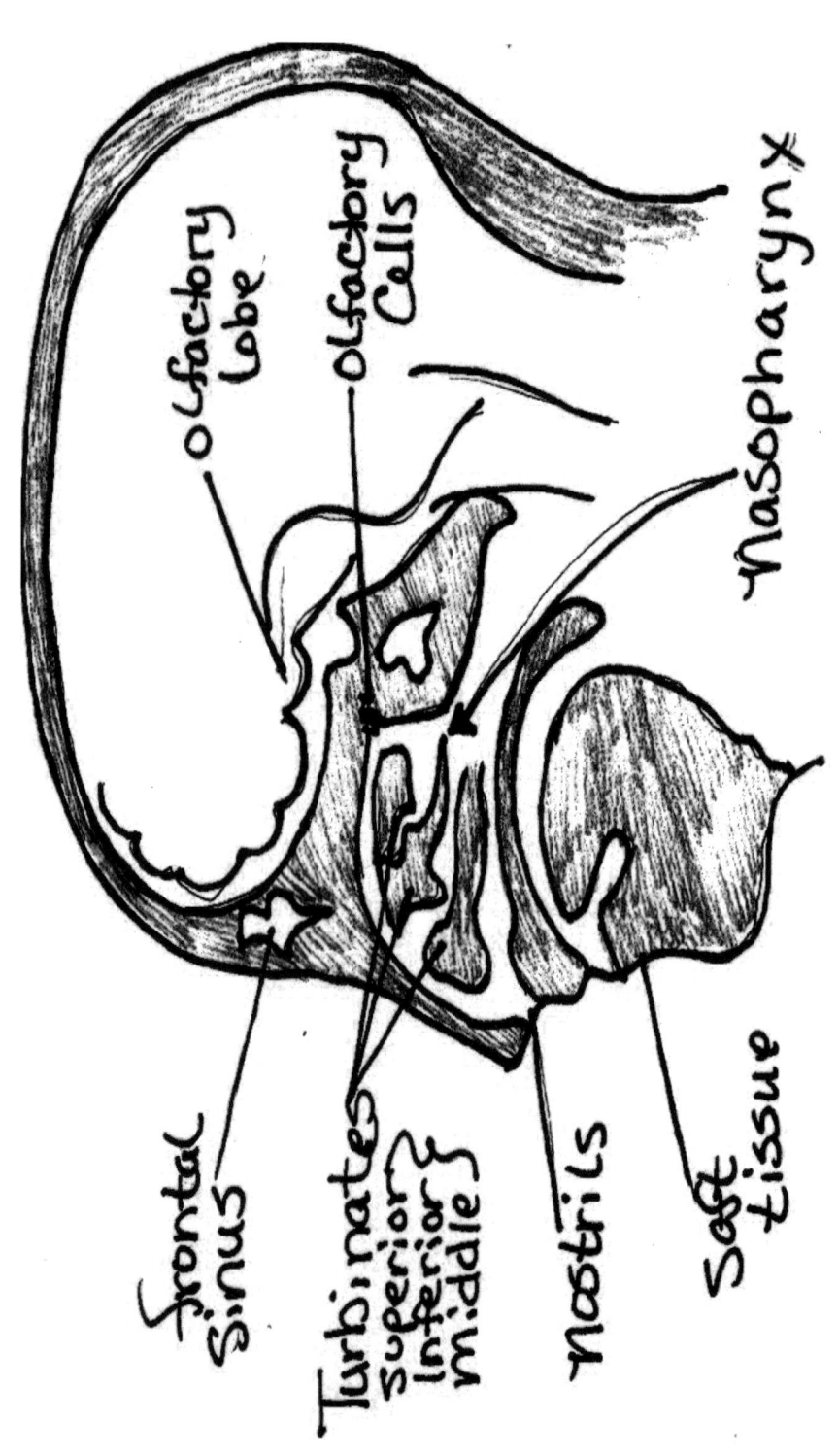

Cells and Skin

The basic constituent of every living thing is the cell. The cell has two parts: (a) nucleus– containing the genetic material DNA, and (b) the cytoplasm– the surrounding semi fluid of proteins and enzymes. Bounding the cytoplasm is the cell membrane which keeps the cell contents in an the undesirables out, yet permits passage of both proper nutrients and waste. The heart of the cell, nevertheless, is the nucleus containing the DNA, which imports individual differences by the manner in which it controls the cell's activities.

The human body is made up of approximately 60 trillion cells. Cells, on the other hand, have a definite life span. For example, epithelial cells (of the skin) last approximately 36 hours, Villi cells (of the intestine) last 43 hours, certain white blood cells live 13 days, red blood cells last 120 days, and nerve cells can live 100 years. It is estimated that 50 million cells die, in or on our body, every second. Many are shed to our environment.

Of the variety of cells and variety of functions, the main concern is the epidermis (skin cells). The skin is about 3/16 of an inch thick, has the ability to regenerate itself, and is the radiator or retainer of heat. It can disclose a nutritional deficiency or glandular malfunction, the presence of a fever, a common infection, or age. The topmost layer is called the epidermis. Under the epidermis is the stratum germinativum, which is constantly pushing new cells upward to replace dead and dying cells on top. Beneath that is the dermis.

Dead cells (rafts) from the skin, the respiratory tract, and digestive tract are constantly shed from the body. The "rafts" of the skin are readily visible to the naked eye, especially on dark, rough fabrics rubbed against the skin.

Skin Secretions

Skin glands contribute their secretions to the environment of the skin surface in the form of sweat, oil, mucous, and other glandular secretions.

Sweat

Sweat is one of the basic contributors to individual body odors. Sweat discharged from the skin is an important consideration in heat regulation and the moisture provided to bacterial residents. It is influenced by the general health of the skin and several environmental factors. Blood vessels in the skin provide water to the epidermis in order to produce cooling by evaporation from the skin surface. It is interesting to note that absorption of water by the skin is a slow process, but the discharge of water is quite rapid. Under average conditions, the accepted amount of discharge, over a 24 hour period, is between 31-50 ounces. The process is constantly at work.

The composition of sweat varies from one individual to the next. The components are so small in amount that they are not categorized by percentage. The chemical constituents are chlorine, sodium, iodine, potassium, urea, calcium, magnesium, phosphate, sulphate, nitrogen compounds, bicarbonate, lipids, sugar and its metabolites, vitamins and hormones.

The sources of sweat are eccrine sweat gland and the apocrine sweat gland. It is necessary to discuss each separately as the secretions differ and the locations vary.

Eccrine Sweat Gland

These glands cover the entire body. Areas most rich with these glands are the forehead, the palms and the axilla. They are most essential for thermoregulation, therefore, heat is the main stimulus. Emotional stress may also produce widespread secretions. Highly spiced foods may induce reflex sweating on the face. Eccrine sweat may occur in large quantities, such as several thousand cc's per hour. The eccrine sweat gland produces a weak saline solution containing nitrogenous substances and other protein material along with heavy concentration of enzymes. Physically, it is clear and a watery secretion.

Apocrine Sweat Glands

The apocrine sweat gland is situated at the base of the hair follicles in particular areas. They are normally found in the areas of the axillae, areolae of the nipples, perinumbilical (navel), perianal, and genital region. They are rather specialized in nature in that secretions are enhanced in response ot stresses such as fear or apprehension. Adult individuals vary considerably in their capacity for apocrine sweating. There is no demonstratable apocrine function in prepubertal children and very old people. The main constituents of apocrine sweat are protein, carbohydrates and ammonia. These are produced slowly and stored until stress. Much offensive body odor is the result of apocrine sweat and resident bacteriologic flora. To test

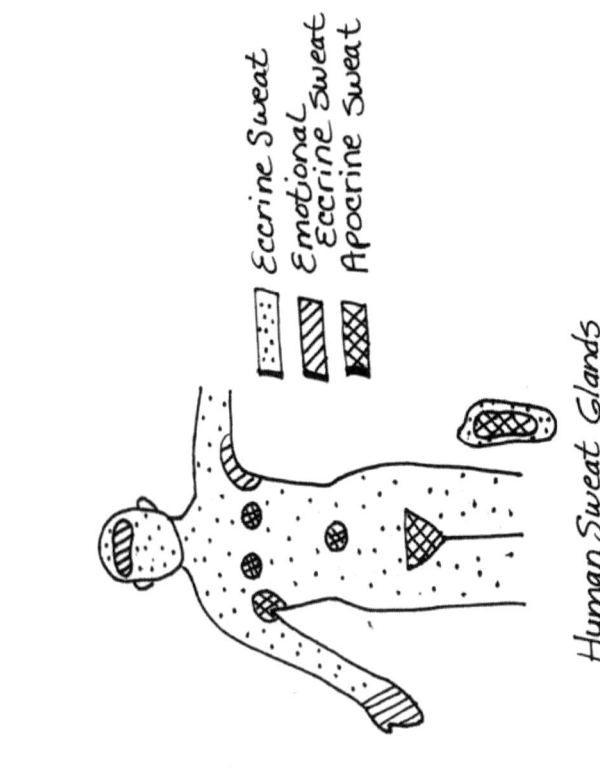

this, samples of sterile apocrine sweat were taken and examined at one hour, six hours, 24 hours, and then once daily. After 14 days there was no perceptible order. However, bacterially contaminated samples produced a perceptible odor within six hours. It is of significance, then, that apocrine secretions are essentially sterile and odorless as they emerge on the skin. Furthermore, in the absence of apocrine sweating, the axilla does not have the strong characteristic odor that is the basis of the deodorant industry. The introduction of apocrine sweat acts as a catalyst, hydrating the bacterial colony which raises the odor in a comparatively short time to a level perceptible to humans.

Hair Follicle and Sebaceous Gland

The greatest abundance of sebaceous glands are found on the face, scalp, upper trunk and pubic area. All hair follicles have an associated sebaceous gland, but some sebaceous glands open directly to the skin. Secretions from these glands, called sebum, spread over the skin surface and mix with the other secretions. There are area differences in sebum formation that vary with age and individual. Sebum has a high proportion of fatty substances.

Other Body Secretions

Other body secretions may contribute substantially to odor, in particular, the respiratory tract and genitourinary tract. These areas also have bacterial populations. The respiratory tract constantly sheds cells. Some cells are exhaled and others are coughed up with mucous. We are all aware of the syndrome "bad breath" much of which results from bacterial activity in the mouth. The genitor-urinary tract secretions have distinctive odors of their own. In addition, if they accumulate, bacterial action will make them much more noticeable. Infections with pathogenic bacteria will produce an even different spectrum of odors.

Inhabitants

One of the major effects of environment on the body id the large population of microorganisms which inhabit it: bacteria, fungi, and parasites. The dominant residents of the skin surface are bacteria which vary both in density and type. Some individuals have a consistently high count while others are low. The denser areas are the face, neck, axilla (arm pits and groin) . The bacteria community of the sole of the foot and between the toes is large.

Summary

Human beings are made up of cells and vapors which are individual through heredity, diet, emotion, metabolism, environment, experience, and bacterial flora. Cells within our body have a definite life span, and epidermis is constantly being replaced. Body odor is produced by the bacteria acting upon dead cells, residues, and body secretions. Added to this activity is the use of soaps. Laundry detergents, deodorants and the individuals reactions to these components. Human odor is undoubtedly very complex and very individualized. There is probably a basic odor which is typical of each individual in good health and normal circumstance. This, in turn, can likely be varied somewhat by emotions, toiletries, clothing and diet. These complex interactions alone can account for millions of variations of human odor.

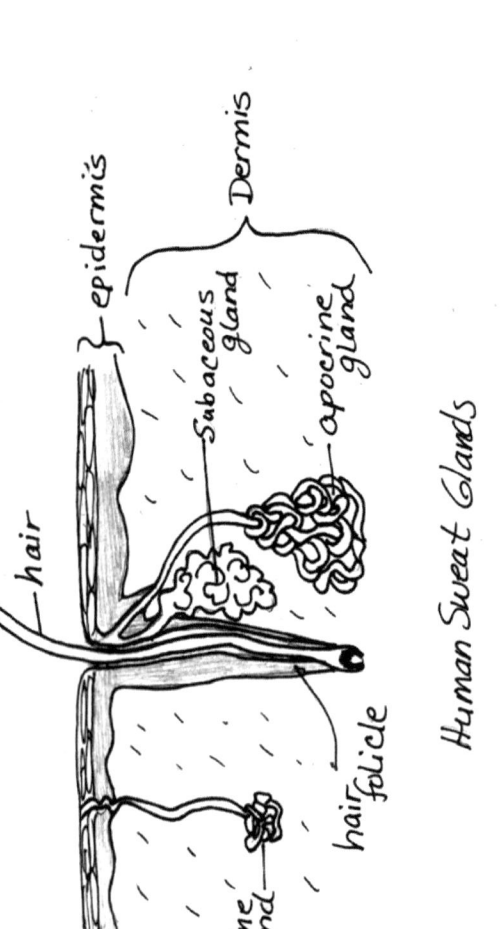

Rafts

We are aware of the stratum germenatvum pushing upward to replace the surface dead cells. This mechanism is constantly at work. Recent research done by R. Davis and W. Noble has shed light on the transmission of staphylococci on tiny "rafts" of skin. Furthermore, these rafts are capable of carrying up to four viable microbial units. Though this work is concerned with medical research to explain airborne transmission of disease, it equally explains how human odor can leave the body and then linger in the environment for many hours.

The rafts are, on the average, 14 microns (.014 mm) in size. The approximate weight is .07 micrograms (.0000000245 oz) They are a cornflake shape which gives them an aerodynamic characteristic. They carry, on the average, four microbial passengers. The raft may be composed of one or more cells. The skin surface has approximately two billion cells, of which 1/30 are being shed daily. This works out to be about 40,000 cells shed by the body each minute.

The idea of shedding minute particles of the skin is not new; however, the consideration of their being bacteria laden was being over looked by most. This raft that is specific to this individual, carrying bacteria and catalyzed by body secretions, enshrouded by the resultant vapor, is undoubtedly very individualized and very identifiable by its little vapor cloud. The scent will continue to be emitted while the nutrients and moisture last.

Body Air Current

It was originally thought that rafts just fell from a person. Recent studies by J. Lewis and co-workers have shown a
current of air next to the skin surface. This provides a rapid transportation system, the estimated speed of which is 125 feet per minute (1.42 mph) it begins at the feet and travels up the legs, slows down under the arms, eddies under the chin, speeds up following the curve of the face and then takes off like a plume from the top of the head. The final dispersion is about 1.52 feet above the persons head. The velocity increases as the outside temperature decreases.

Clothes in some cases, accelerated the velocity. Heavy exercise followed by loosening of the collar resulted in a bellows effect around the neck region. The air trapped within the shirt surges up and over the subjects head. Clothes, then, do not substantially alter the flow of air even though the clothing styles are different. This particular research project came forth with the interesting possibility that during the time a person is taking a shower, the upward flow of air is disrupted by the water moving in a downward direction. This, in turn, caused scattering effect of the air currents with a subsequent increase in migrating rafts immediately afterward. So, while a shower may temporarily decrease the odorous substances on the skin, the rate of shedding scent is increased. The net effect of altering personal scent is probably very brief.

The important feature is that the study of the body air currents provides a transportation system for the bacteria laden rafts. Furthermore, it is a method that launches these rafts at a high rate of speed.

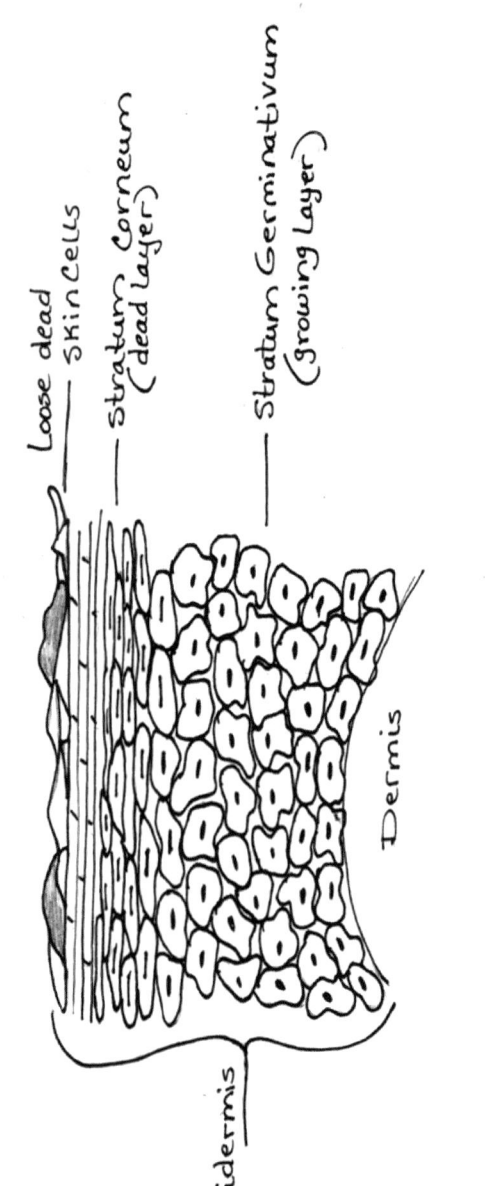

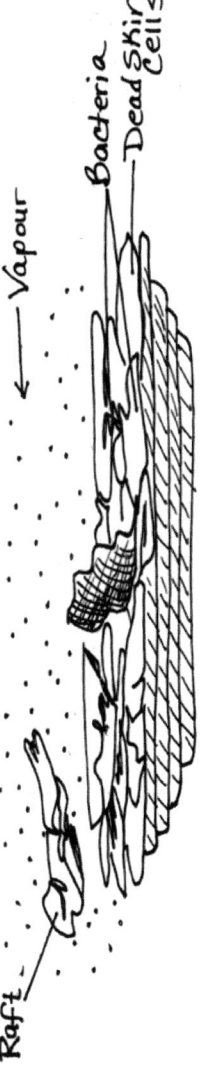

Shedding of Dead Skin Cells

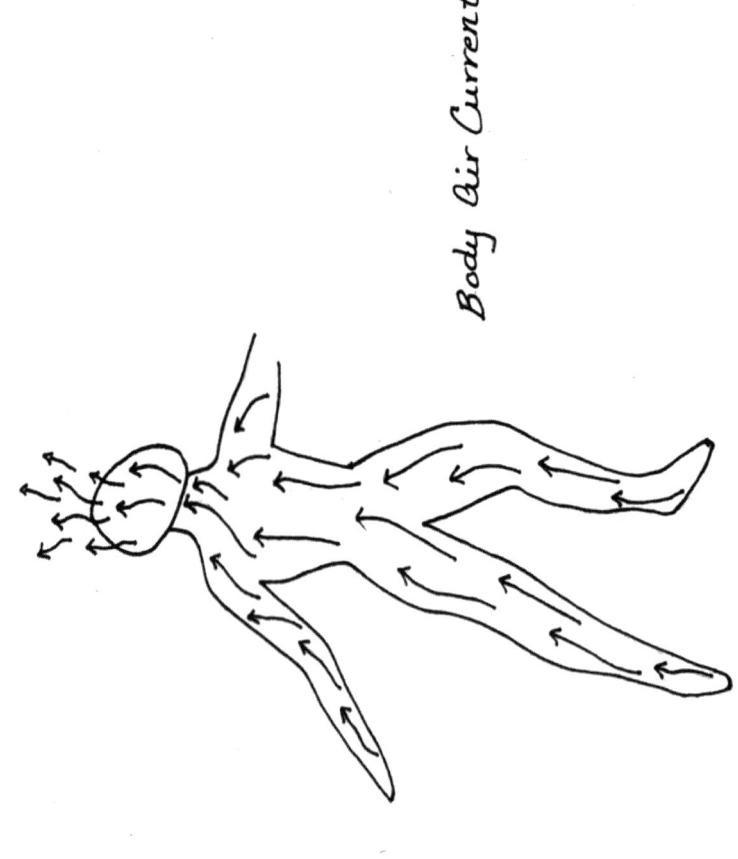

Chemical Analysis of Individualistic Scent

Some people try to break down the scent into a single or near single component. Scent can not be broken down this way. On a modular basis, scent is composed of a combination of many elements. Few dog handlers are chemists and don't realize that an atom can completely change a molecule of a particular substance. For example, two atoms of hydrogen combined with oxygen constitutes water (H_2O); however 2 atoms of hydrogen combined with one atom of sulfur makes hydrogen sulfide (H_2S) Hydrogen sulfide smells like rotten eggs, one atom different than water and a huge change in odor.

Let us entertain some possibilities. First consideration was bacteria acting upon skin secretions. Therefore, let us break down these secretions into eight basic chemicals that we know thus far. They are chlorine, sulfate, sodium, potassium, magnesium, phosphate, and iodine, not counting the nitrogen compounds, etc. If we were consider these eight, two at a time, we can calculate 56 different combinations, three at a time, we have 336 different combinations; eight at a time, we have 40,320 different combinations. If we introduce the eight different ingredients and five different bacteria, we then have 13 variables with which to work. Taken two at a time, we then have 6,227,020,800. it should be recognized that we have more than 13 variables available, thus the number of combinations almost goes to infinity.

Is this enough to account for individuality? Mathematically, yes. We have enough different combinations to account for the worlds present population with enough left over to accommodate the population growth for many years to come.

Discriminatory Evidences

When one looks at the total ground picture the humanoid evidences are the raft vapors. Some rafts may fall very close to the footstep, but the majority will be dispersed over a wide area depending on the wind. If a person walks at a rate of three miles an hour, there will be approximately 151 rafts per foot deposited along his route. It should also be remembered that these rafts are very small, thus the scent is not long lasting and may go through different intensity levels. However, these rafts, only a few of which fall near footsteps, are the humanoid evidences and provide the information for discriminating one human from another.

As we know, not all search and rescue dogs are capable of finding missing persons alive. Sometimes we hear of dogs searching within feet of a missing person but passing right by them. Search dogs tracking capability is subdivided into "Disturbance Tracking" and "Scent Discrimination Tracking." Disturbance tracking is just that - following the most recent disturbance not a specific scent. Criminals when they leave a crime scene or scared lost people are exuding adrenalin that canines, can be trained to track. Disturbed grass or tracks in the ground is another example. This is the most common type of trailing dog used in law enforcement. Search and Rescue dogs are also used as trailing dogs because we often arrive on scenes where we have no scent articles. There is no specific scent we want them to follow except the tracks they find in the ground disturbance.

Scent discrimination Tracking is following a specific scent of skin cells that are constantly being given off from every person even at rest. Only a select few dogs possess the capacity for this specialized work. Bloodhounds can not only discriminate scents, but they also have the ability to catalog up to three scents at a time and are capable of being trained for "scent discrimination tracking." Such trained dogs have been known to follow a skin cell trail down the middle of roads that are given off through the air circulation vent of the car the subject is traveling in.

During a test performed to demonstrate this by Bob Borden in Cody, Wyoming, several people were put out in the middle of a field. A canine handler that proclaimed to have a dog that could catalog human scent was going to show how her golden lab was able to perform such a task. Bob Borden picked three individuals to go away from the group and go hide from the start point about 150 meters out. Each person that hid left a scent article behind for Bob to present to the handler. Once the three hiders were down and hiding, the group of people moved out of the area. Bob picked a scent article of one of the hiders and properly presented it to the handler telling her that her dog needed to find the person that belonged to that article. She confidently took her dog out to where the group of people had been and presented her dog the article. The dog started casting back and forth as if looking for that very scent and then took off tracking, quickly finding the wrong hider. The handler tried several more times and each time the dog returned to the first track it had found and was unsuccessful at discriminating which human it was supposed to find. Most likely the dog was like all other trailing dogs and had learned by ground disturbance, get on a track and stay on it, oldest scent to newest scent. The handler was confused saying she had even tested her dog and was certified by a SAR organization in doing just this. Once she explained that the test was set up so that only the person whom her dog was to find was left in the field, all others that had tracked it up were gone, it explained the situation perfectly! All dogs are capable of air scenting and if you always train with a live person at the end then that's how you should be testing. However, ALL the people must be left there in order to truly see if your dog is cataloging scent or just simply air scenting a human. The same test given to a bloodhound and no one leaving the field provided an accurate picture of how this works. Seventeen people standing in a group, the bloodhound was given three scented socks of three of the individuals in the group. The bloodhound meticulously picked out the right people in the group for the scent articles he was given...in the right order!

What kind of dog do I have?

The differences in search dogs come in a few different categories. For the sake of this book, we talk about the trailing, tracking and air scent dog. A cadaver dog or evidence detecting dog could be classified as an air scenting dog as they train in similar ways but with different scent objectives. A diagram of how these dogs work differently is on the next page. We can see how the tracking dog moves along on the track, nose down, there is not much room for error here. This dog will find all evidence on the trail too if trained to alert to that as well. The Air scent dog will pick their head up and head into the scent that is carried on the wind, often ignoring the ground disturbance completely. The air scent dog will find the victim faster on most occasions but will not find any evidence left on the track. Then there is the trailing dog. The trailing dog applies both tactics, they will put their nose down and track, pick it up and scent and they wonder all over the tracks as they pick up the scents scattered around by the victim. They will stay remarkably close to the track but wont be on it for long. This dog can miss evidence but might find it as well. This is one of the most common search dogs being run today. Benefits of this type of dog would be the ability to track and air scent, they can often be used in both capacities. It is my belief however that all search dogs need to begin with the fundamentals of tracking to begin. I have seen excellent air scent dogs that began this way and so –so dogs that started with hide and go seek rather than tracking or trailing training them first.

Air Currents

Understanding how the air we train in can change where we think scent should be traveling is a huge concern. Look at the diagrams on the next several pages to help understand how air currents and scent travels. Training your K9 with all different types of environmental concerns in mind will benefit your progress as a whole. If you can, try and train in several conditions. Wet, dry, windy, and everything in between. Knowing how to predict where the scent is traveling will greatly increase your success in training your dog and actually performing complex searches.

Strong Winds vs. Light Wind

A subjects scent can move a great distance in a strong wind, however, the scent will be more concentrated in a stream like pattern as it moves along quickly and with force. A light wind will dissipate more to the sides in a fanning type pattern but still carry for a good distance. This can often make it even harder to detect the actual area the victim might be in if the scent is spreading out a lot. Don't ever be afraid to train in a strong wind. Once your dog is doing good in great conditions, its time to start throwing in the hard stuff.

Scent Pooling

When scent is "stuck" in a low area or circles into an area over an obstruction we get what is known as scent pooling. This can make the scent highly concentrated in this area and we may find our dogs circling and unable to come out of the area on the actual trail. Once you determine the wind, obstacle, etc and how your dog is acting in this area, try moving the dog out in a sweeping motion to get them out of the pool and into the air current again. This will allow your dog to pick up again on the track.

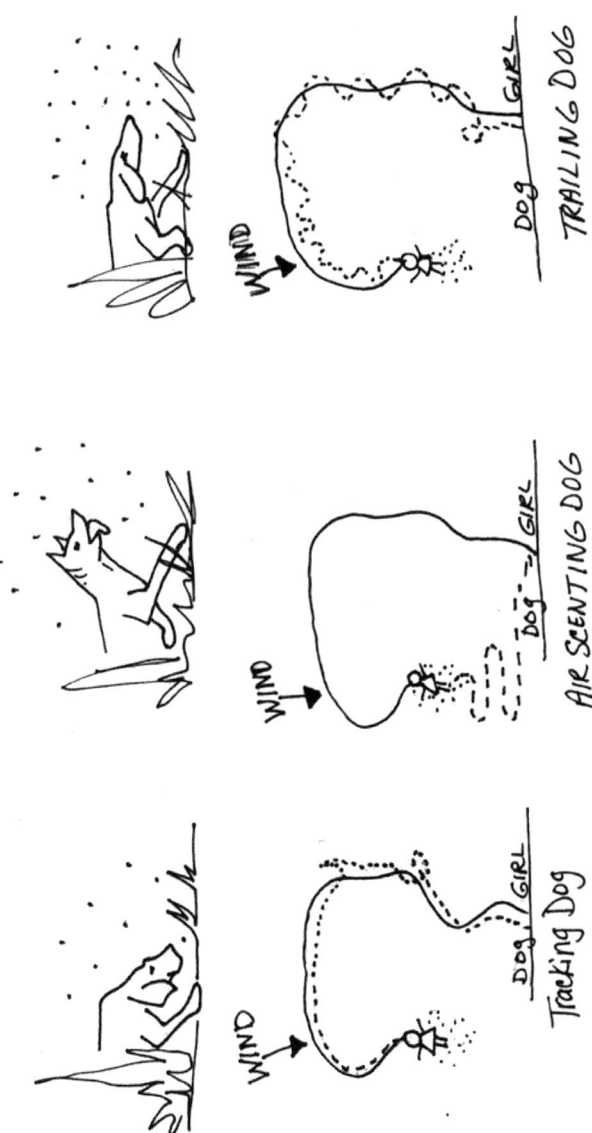

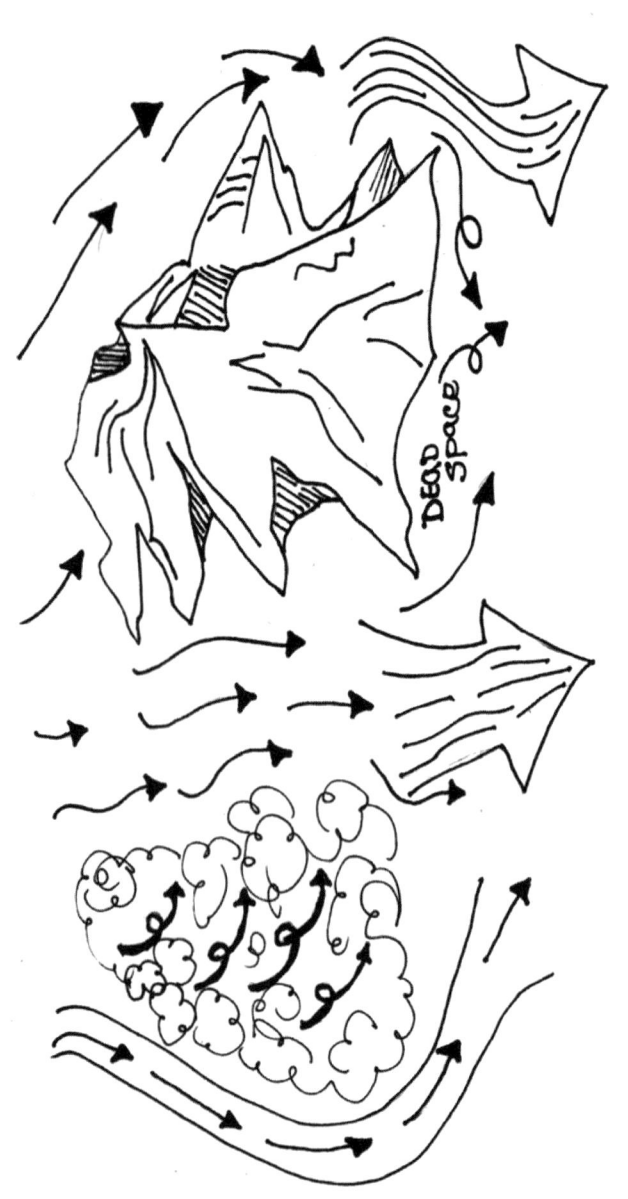

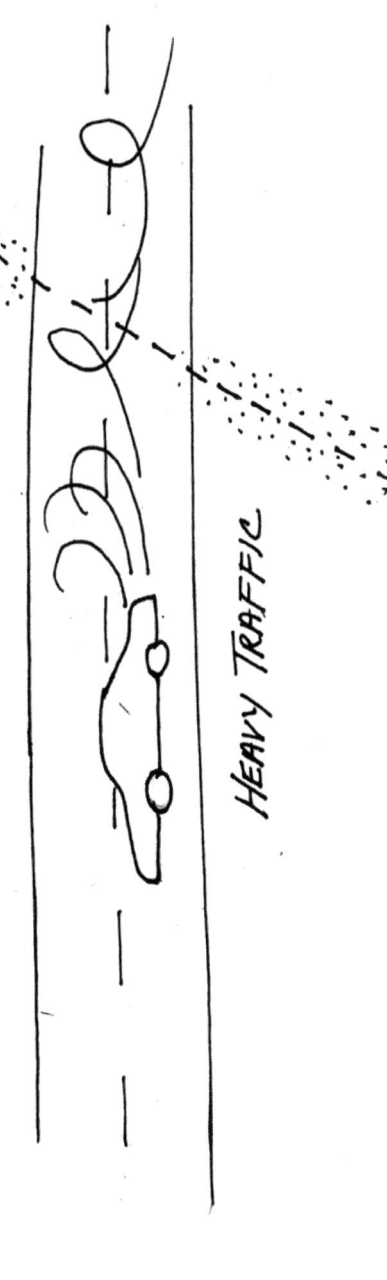

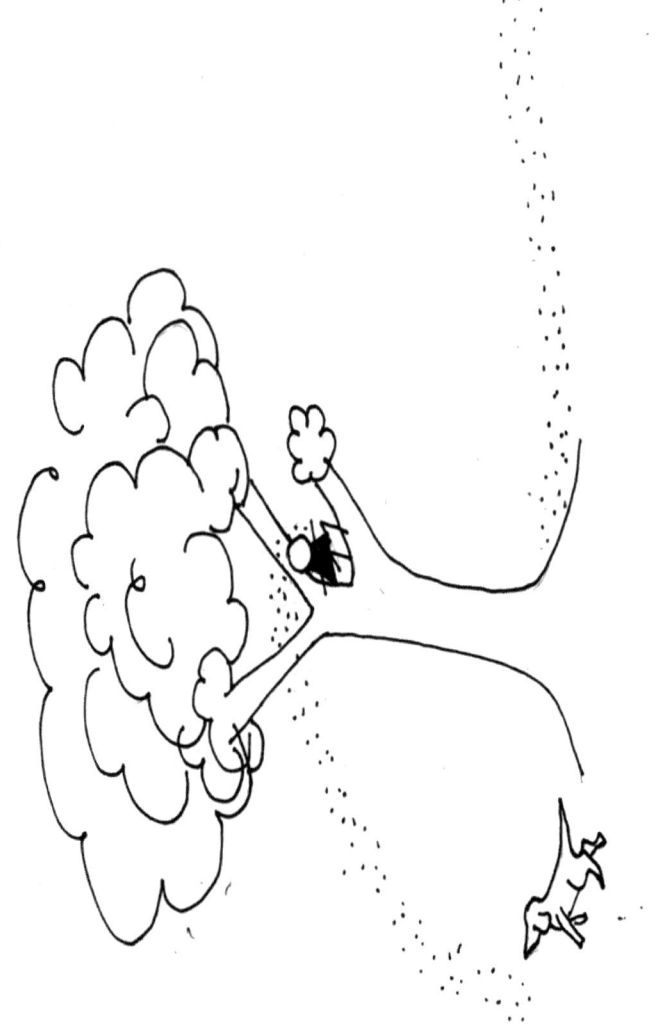

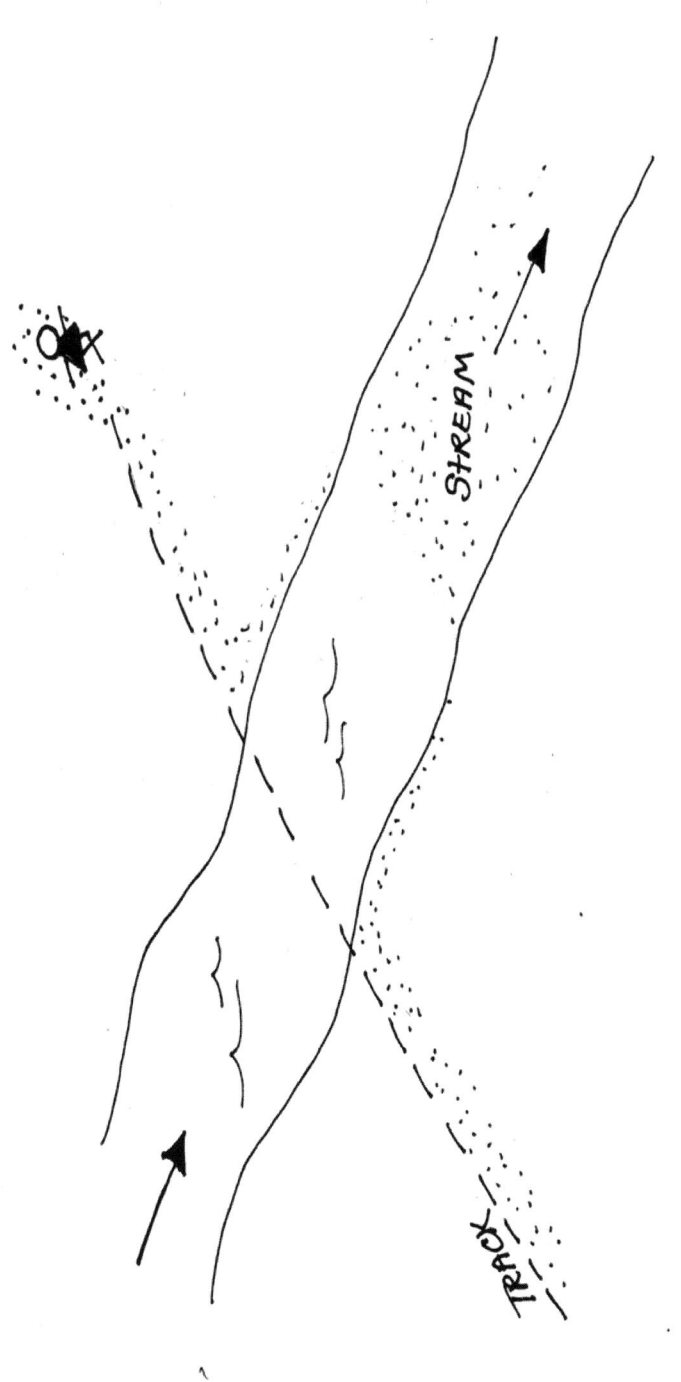

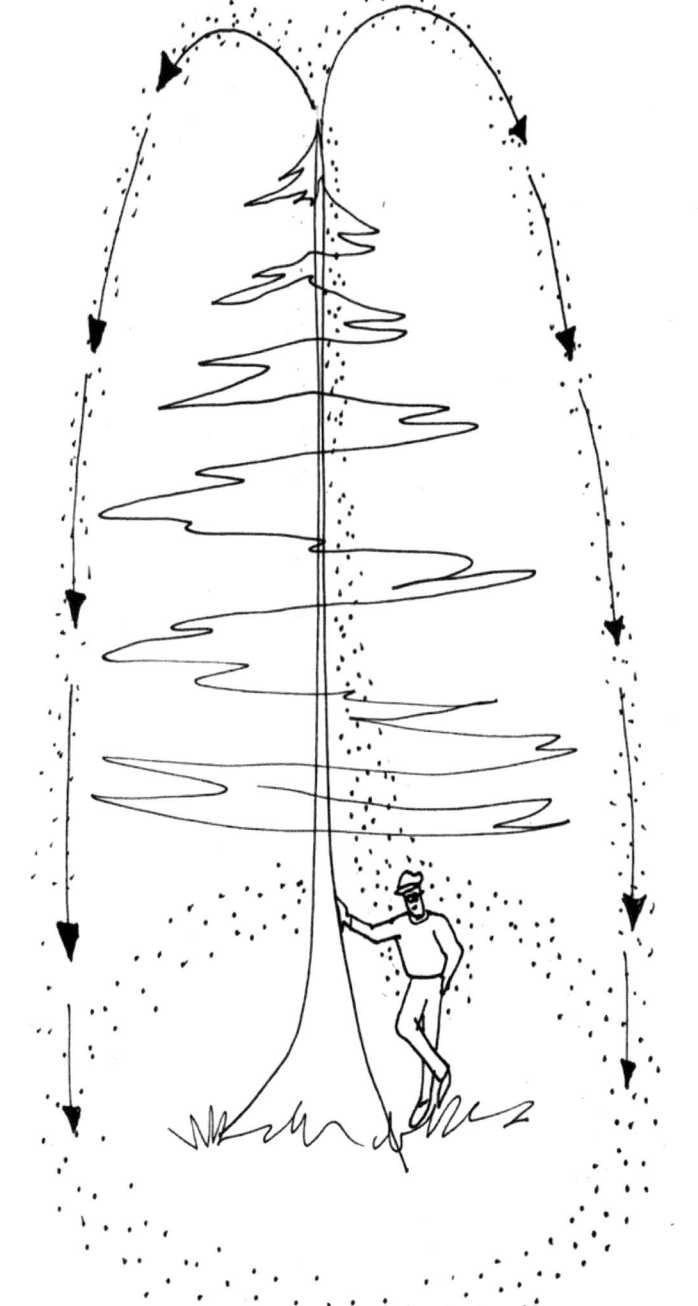

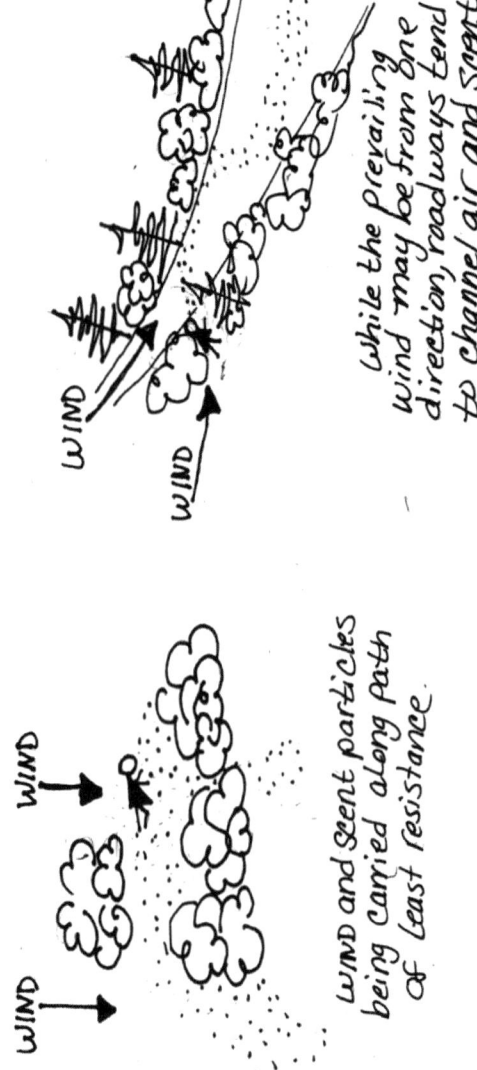

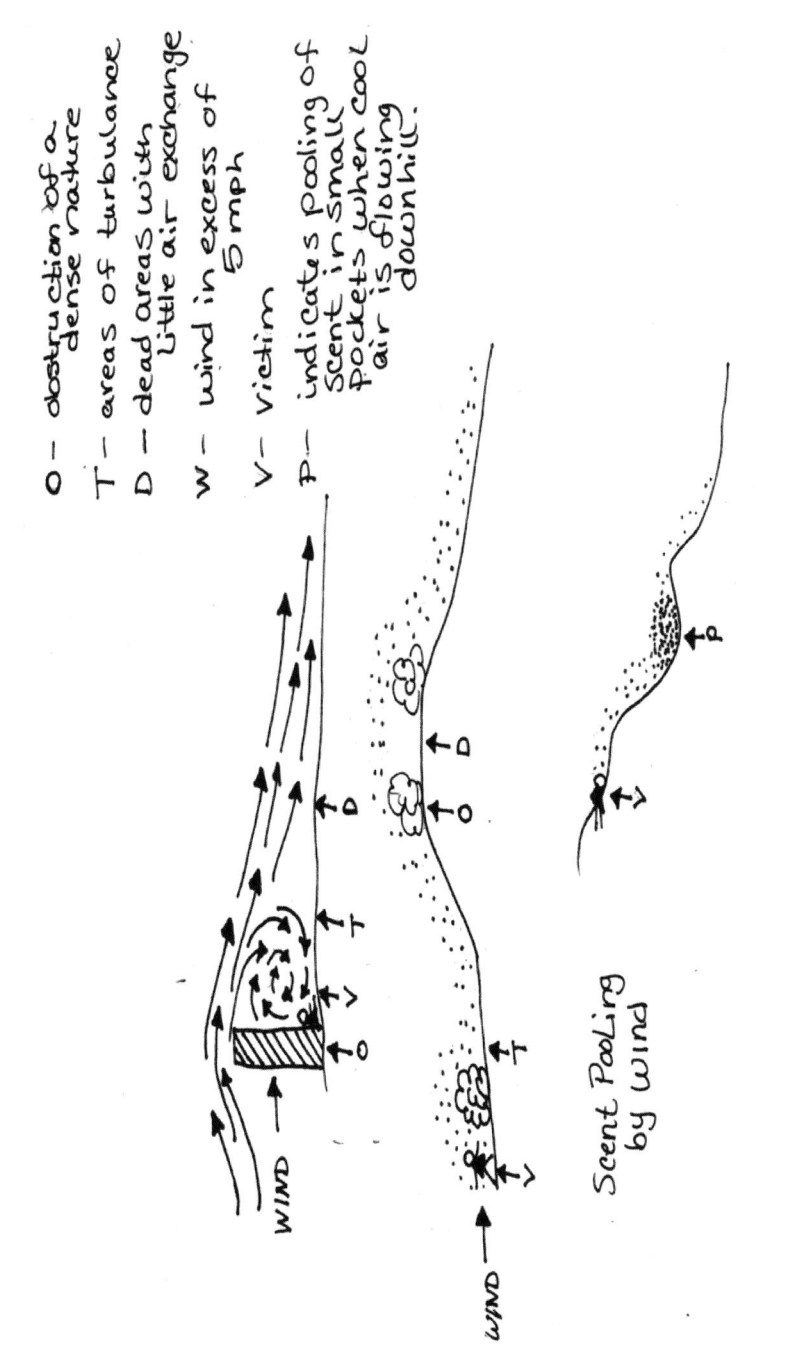

Bibliography and Suggested Readings

Chiacchia PhD, Kenneth (2000). "In Search of Human Scent." *Advanced Rescue Technology, October/November,* 24 - 30.

Syrotuck, William (1972). Scent and the Scenting Dog (3rd Edition). Arner Publishing.

Pearsall, Milo and Verbruggen M.D., Hugo (1982). Scent. Alpine Publications.

Puttnam, Clare (1991). "Science: Can Police Dogs Really Sniff Out Criminals." *New Scientist, 1786.*

Leffingwell PhD, John (2002). "Olfaction - Update No. 5." *Leffingwell Reports, Vol. 2 (No. 1), May 2002).* Leffingwell & Associates.

CPSIA information can be obtained
at www.ICGtesting.com
Printed in the USA
LVIW011425171012
303291LV00001B